# REDISCOVER YOUR MAGIC

## How to Energetically Align Your Path and Calling to Bring your Ideas to Life

## LILY NICHOLSON

Cover Design: Lily Nicholson

Interior: Lily Nicholson

Paperback ISBN: 978-0-578-77517-3

Published by:

Lily Nicholson / The Pathfinder Code®

**To all of the beautiful souls relentlessly in pursuit of their true calling and aligning it with their path!**

**I see you!**

# GRAB YOUR FREE GIFT!

Do you want to get a head start to ***Rediscover Your Magic*** and bring your ideas to life? Of course, you do! You are on a journey of self-discovery!

This Pathfinder Code® E-Guide **Energetically Align Your Path with Your Calling** is an introduction to the concept of learning to read your own internal compass and guide yourself through your biggest questions and decisions. So, you can connect with what you really want, find direction and live life on your own extraordinary terms.

Here's what you need to do:

1. Go to my **Contact Page** at www.thepathfindercode.com
2. Click on the image of the E-Guide and tell us where to email the access link.
3. Check your email, then download the PDF.

# CONTENTS

## FOREWARD

There are times in life you come across a person with a unique spark, a special gift in the way they see the world and a determination to spread their magic.

Lily Nicholson is one of those people. Upon meeting her a few years ago, I immediately recognized her intuition and compassion for others, not to mention her creative and artistic talent.

I had the opportunity to talk with her in person for hours over those next few days and will never forget how wonderful it felt to be "seen" for the first time in a very long time.

Lily is here to create a beautiful legacy in the world and help so many others do the same. It's about so much more than her own dreams and experiences… it's a treasure trove of lessons, the effect they can have on others, the way they relate and resonate, and the way she helps you unleash what you have within.

I recall witnessing her jump out of her own comfort zone with the undeniable determination to do what she was born to and help so many others do it too, in their own way, with their own reason and rhyme. I knew at that moment, that the sparkle in her eyes would move mountains.

Two years before this book was even written, I saw that spark, the determination, and the magic. I can recall how I knew, not thought or hoped, but just knew without a doubt that this woman would change lives in a profound and magnificent way.

Her explanation of how people can change their mindset, unleash their truth, find the path that brings them fulfillment and happiness, and live a life they love is something I too believe in. Lily has a beautiful way of expressing it, helping others achieve it, and making an exquisite and magical mark in the world.

This book is for anyone looking to rediscover what ignites their spark, to thrive in the life they feel meant for… for those who know and believe they have unleashed magic inside of them that can add color to the world, a shimmer, a glitter, a change or a splash of light into lives that feel dim.

I hope you enjoy and use your own magic to move mountains and be the beautiful soul you that you were born to be.

*Cassandra Lennox*
*Author, Poet & Creator of "The Inspiration Chain"*

# PREFACE

Working for yourself is part of the "The American Dream" isn't it?

The physical and financial freedom we imagine having is definitely the No. 1 "shiny object" that bedazzles most, if not all, aspiring entrepreneurs.

Why is this? I have come to learn, that the "spell" cast on or over us is far more alluring and romantic than a joy stealing day job. The job where you clock in, every day, so you can pay your bills while helping to build someone else's dreams.

Wherever you find yourself today, I invite you to reflect on the richness of your experiences.

Do not underestimate the value they have had on your inner wisdom. There is a sweetness about our experiences that we tend to overlook. We must sift through what we once viewed as "ordinary" and look at it through the lens of the "extraordinary". To the YOU, yes YOU, reading this book.

Have you have fallen in love with the idea of being an entrepreneur? If so, some rewiring of how you think has already taken place.

You get intuitive nudges that spark you in ways that haunt you...until you listen. These nudges used to keep me up at night. Until, they didn't.

Once upon a time, my original ideas resided at the crossroads of where I was, and where I wanted to be.

There came a day, where I could no longer sit at the edge of my dreams and watch my *beloved* die a slow death. The "beloved" I speak of here are my original ideas and passion to help others.

These ideas were the ones that I not only fell in love with many years ago. They were the ones that lit me up from the inside out!

Some mentors "advised" me that a mix of my ideas would not work and that I had to pick only one!

This is the part of the big "why" of this book.

For all the times I listened to this so- called advice.

For all the times I stopped believing in myself for even a nano second.

No matter which moment I was in, I questioned everything.

There was nothing magical in this space of being.

The heaviness of my day job in Law seemed to be louder than my inner voice at times. I wondered if my magic had eluded me somehow. Derailed, for a moment? Nope! In reality, it was many months. This is why I am super compelled to share this story. It's not mine to withhold.

You see, a celebration was in order! I advocated for myself, with myself. I learned how to silence both the internal and external chatter. The noise and the naysayers. Goodbye!

Why would I settle for a second-hand version of the life I had fallen in love with, when I was born for greatness! You were too.

What did you think was inside this book when you read the title?

Did you feel the jolt? The butterflies that I did while writing it?

My name is Lily Nicholson. I am the founder of The Pathfinder Code® Powered by Intuition and Creativity. I am an Intuitive Life & Success Coach.

I help entrepreneurs find their voice, their next right path and bring their ideas to life. The results are they *energetically align their path and calling.*

What could be more magical than this while building your own dream?

I am also that woman who fell in love with the vision of what I will coin as my "new now" with open arms. My new now had danced in my head for many years.

Until, I accepted my own invitation to embrace my beloved. Yes, that beloved is me and the original ideas that I birthed. You too, have your own beloved. Do you see her? How long has it been since you looked into her eyes and the depths of her soul?

Yes, I ask lots of questions! Stay with me until the very last page of this book! I promise it will be worth it! There you will be rewarded with the energetic tools to empower you, to create your "new now" and Rediscover Your Magic!

For decades I worked at law firms in a corporate environment. Yes, there it is, the joy-stealing day job. Was this the *alleged* demise of my magic! Not exactly! You see, I am grateful for this job as it supported my vision and mission. Yes, it pays the bills.

How did I get here? Glad you asked. There was a time when this lit me up. I am not one to do things that do not interest me.

In my early legal career, much of my day, included writing, both persuasive and creative. These opportunities that used to spark my passion for justice and equality, disappeared. So did my interest. As I write this, I have a firm exit date planned. It's on my calendar. Events on my calendar happen, that is why they are placed there! It is this exit plan and this vision, that fuels my desire to continue to embrace my "beloved."

I am also a self-taught visual artist with a creative business that I love; the polar opposite of my career in law.

One thing I know for sure…my artistry and the call to create and help others has kept my sanity on multidimensional levels.

It was through a self-discovery process that I identified three core values. These values have formed the foundation of my vision and mission in The Pathfinder Code®.

1. *Creating*- Honoring my original ideas and imagination.

2. *Investigating*- Listening to what my intuition is signaling me to do, or not do, and what I allow to influence me.

3. *Speaking up*- Using my voice to articulate on my own behalf and own my personal power.

***Note: You have core values too! *Grab a piece of paper and a pen and take a moment and write them down! You will come back to these later in the book!**

I have learned to better understand myself and become more self-aware through my own processes.

This has been part of the magic that evolved in my "do it herself" energetic toolkit while building my intuitive empire to empower other entrepreneurs.

Yes, there are many things I do myself, but, know this, even the best of the best, need a coach to level up.

I hired not one, but several to assist me in this adventure! This was one of the most life-changing decisions I ever made.

Knowing my core values has helped me to "align" my insight with my actions. This alignment is different for everyone. My experience over time, developed into a rhythm. The ebb and flow of this rhythm was conveyed to me in a language that I learned to understand and it soon became my North Star. Especially, on those days where I questioned my magic. That language was my intuition and creativity.

I am a visionary, a dreamer and a lover of the planet and its people.

I know I am this and so much more. So are YOU!

I thrive on the mystery and the perceived magnificence that awaits me on the other side of my ideas. The lure of this somewhat elusive intangible. I see it as the "not yet done" or the "undone".

This notion of "undone" is twofold. It will either motivate or trigger "frustration". Did you know, that frustration has its positive attributes? While the underlying emotions don't feel good, they force us to find the tools we need to thrive. This is a common story line among the women I have coached.

Despite the frustration, these women, were in love with the notion of living life on their own terms. The vision and alignment to their "new now" was far too fulfilling in their mind's eye to quit.

"Alignment" is the sweet spot where your thoughts and words intersect. It's the magical portal where the "doing" of the bold action is a catalyst for transformation, the ultimate reward!

In business, "alignment" calls on us to present our expert knowledge to our ideal clients. Please know that this book is not about linear thinking, in fact, it's quite the opposite!

It's more about "energetic alignment" with the path you find yourself on now. Then investigating the path and co-creating improvements along the way.

As a self-taught visual artist, I would never settle to color inside the lines that anyone draws. Ever. I came here to be me. You, came here to be YOU.

To rediscover your magic, I will tag ideas or actions that would be more useful for you to have "turned on". I will also tag the ones that I recommend you "turn off"! The choice is yours, as are the results you will get while on this journey with me!

The *idea of* ***Rediscover Your Magic*** was born out of my desire to be able to read my own internal compass and guide myself through my biggest questions and decisions.

The practices I share in this book are from my life experience, my creative and coaching businesses and learning how to connect with what I really wanted. All of these practices have worked for myself, my clients and can work for you too!

My goal as an Intuitive Life and Success Coach is to teach others the game-changing techniques for busting through energetic, emotional and creative blocks and help them nurture and bring their original ideas to life.

If you are ready to bust through the myth that you were somehow talked out of your magic, then know, that this book is the creative cure!

Drawing on the visual discovery techniques, mindfulness practices and self-love, *Rediscover Your Magic* helps you unblock your intuition and creativity and lets your true gifts and talents shine through! See you on the other side of building your own dreams!

# INTRODUCTION

## *TURNING OFF THE INNER CRITIC!*

Let's start this journey with some housekeeping! The first order of business is "turning off the chatter of your inner critic". Yes, you have one, I have one, we all have one. We can deny it until the moon turns blue. It's a simple truth, that once accepted, it is very empowering.

To overthrow the inner critic's hold on your thoughts, your *inner voice* must be louder and larger than your fears of your inner critic. The fears of what the inner critic will say, think and how *she* makes you feel. You are the sole proprietor of your emotions and your voice. Owning your inner voice is the very first step to rediscover your magic.

On this journey to rediscover your magic you must turn off all distractions. That is, if you are committed and really want this to work for you! Are you?

Next up, turn off the chatter of your social media and the plethora of online "experts". I promise it will serve you. The only voice I want you to hear at this moment is your own as you read this book.

### *FIND YOURSELF IN MY WORDS*

Know that I only ask of you, those things I ask of myself. I want for you, what I want for me.

A short rant here. My only one on this topic. I was hesitant to talk about this but I knew if I didn't, you would not know what to avoid. So, about some of those "experts". They are masters at "bamboozling" personal growth folks and aspiring entrepreneurs. Buyer beware of the painful journey into "drip method" land. This method has a plethora of high vibe words and calls to action. There are moments where they grab your attention for days, months, sometimes years. This process can and will undermine your "experience of yourself" by the way it's delivered. I speak from only from my own experience.

The reason I mention this in connection with the inner critic is twofold. One, this type of experience will take you a year or more to finish, then you will need time to recover. Yes, that *was* my experience, not yours, nor do I want it to be yours. But it would be a disservice to not educate you about what is out there. During my time in such a program, I worked diligently so that my visions would not die a slow death. Had I not worked as hard as I did, I would not be where I am today. Nor would I be writing this book. I write this book from a place of empathy and compassion for my fellow entrepreneurs. I do not want anyone of you, *ever*, to be bamboozled.

So, any calls to action or distractions that resemble the drip method, need to be "turned off", permanently!

The goal of this book is to help you find your voice and rediscover your magic as if we were face to face. This book is to introduce to an alternative personal growth and coaching practice. One where I am personally available for private 1:1 coaching. Yes, you have access to me, by phone, by text, by apps, videoconference and live in-person events. You will be educated and mentored and receive the panoramic view of what breathing fresh ideas into your life and your business can do to help you, rediscover your magic, and turn your ideas into valuable products and services!

Your voice is the internal compass to build your intuitive empire. Getting unstuck means uncovering the myths, the hidden blocks that hold you captive. If there are some spots that need remapping, your heart and brain connection will kick in. It will clear the path for your intuition to signal and direct you to those messages meant for you only. Expect to experience all of this while reading this book.

Today, is the best time to get clarity on your calling.

This is very important work you are doing here and it's your time and your turn, to commit to it.

There is no better story I could share with you. One that tells the tale of what it feels like to align your path and calling.

Did you know, it starts very early in one's life?

An early childhood friend, "Susan" created art as an escape from her family issues. It was her "safe place". Growing up in The Bronx we all needed something to call our own that brought us joy.

There came a point where Susan stopped creating. The negativity and external influences she received crushed her confidence. I remember telling her that she needed to create, that it was her happy place and that I didn't want a grumpy best friend.

She would ask me, "How do you know that this is what I need?" I told her that I could see how it lit her up. It was like she was a light bulb and was completely turned up to the highest wattage possible. In her mind, she was not good at art or anything. She no longer wanted to create. *She felt that people didn't like her, with or without her art.*

What she did not see, was that her art gave her a voice, a way to speak up for herself, a way to express herself without words. It was her path to transformation, back home to herself.

The truth is, Susan was an amazing artist. We would visit for hours. We created magical realms, to wherever our imaginations transported us that particular day. Susan loved to create images of women in beautiful gowns. She aspired to be a fashion designer. She would say then she was older she would do this! She wanted to make dresses for women that made them feel beautiful, inside and out! What I know now, was, that she wanted to help other women feel "seen" rather than invisible. This is how she felt.

She would share at times that while she loved to create art, it made her tired. Susan had some chronic medical issues.

Creating art or doing anything was a daunting and exhausting activity. It pained her as much as it pleasured her. That is *until...*

Susan did return to creating art many years later. I learned that she dedicated her life's work to helping others using her art as a therapeutic tool. The catalyst for her return to art was a canvas and paint her sister gifted her. Her sister told her she had quite enough of Susan's reluctance to do the one thing she loved the most. Her sister was always the wave-maker and peacemaker. I laugh as I write this about my friend. I am still uncertain who was the more relentless, strong-willed child. Susan or her sister with that wise, inner knowing, observing what Susan needed.

Reflecting on my time with Susan. I am sure it was the combination of us co-creating ideas and supporting each other that made our time so magical. We invented, imagined and created our own magic.

We all have within us, the ability to believe in something far larger than our fears.

How exactly do we pull this off?

I believe the power is outside of our five senses. I have found in working with other that its more about harnessing the power of our multi-sensory perception. Author Gary Zukav says it best in his book, *Soul Stories*, "Multisensory perception and intuition are the same thing, but multisensory perception is a more accurate name.

Most people think that intuition is a hunch that occurs now and then…it is more than that. It is a very sophisticated system that allows you to see more than you can with your five senses. As we become more and more intuitive, and we all are, we encounter different kinds of these experiences"

For this take place, we need to shift the veil of being on autopilot i.e., the everyday version of us that goes to work and pays the bills. This is the version of us that also, cannot "find the time" to pause to see what is working and what isn't.

There are those that have pulled this off, left the 9 to 5, and have since made it their life's work to help others follow suit.

This "ability" is in everyone and needs to always be "TURNED ON"!

Having someone that cares by your side to co-create the life you desire is essential. Susan had stopped creating because she believed what others said to her about her art was true. She took it personal, because she thought it was. In reality, it was very, very personal. Until, she took the time to re-experience the very thing that she wanted to do, fear was her driver. I received word that Susan passed away last year.

My memories flashed back to that exact moment when Susan returned to her beloved creativity. I could not fathom the thought of her leaving this planet with her magical art still inside her.

This is synchronicity. Energetic alignment of your path with your calling. In this space, you experience who you came here to be and do what you came here to do. This is the highest calling that any human will aspire to carry out while on this 3-D planet.

Can anyone do this? Do you have to be born creative or someone that helps others find their way, or can you learn it?

Again, this book is not just about art and creativity, it's about so much more. I use art as a metaphor often as I find it emulates every experience under the sun.

Keep these unspoken rules in mind as you read this book:

You don't need a degree to help other people.

You don't have to have all the answers to your own questions.

You can learn this and more, and also get the help you need to level up.

You can learn self-trust, and to listen to your heart and intuition.

You can learn to use your voice and believe in what you say about yourself.

You can learn to advocate for yourself, and design how your life will look and feel, today and tomorrow.

You can learn to let nothing stand in the way of what feels like "home" and lights you up from the inside out.

You can learn to START doing and never STOP.

You can learn to use discernment, on what you need to turn on, and what you need to turn off.

Until…another magical idea comes along!

Lather, rinse repeat.

**Decide what will be true for you today, you decide what will be true for you tomorrow**

# CHAPTER 1:
# DO YOU SECOND GUESS YOUR INTUITION?

Intuition: the ability to understand something immediately; a thing that one knows or considers likely from instinctive feeling rather than conscious reasoning (~Oxford Dictionary)

In this book you will come across content that will trigger both your emotions and reasoning.

What if you could navigate your emotions without the "charge" attached to them from the past?

Your path to be successful at this is doing your inner work. I invite you to trust yourself, the self-discovery process and your intuition.

Uncovering hidden emotional blocks is the first step in this self-discovery process.

Next is shining a light on what's holding you back. Left undone, this will paralyze you from doing your life's work. It will desensitize you so that "killing off your original ideas" is the new normal.

When we second guess our intuition, we battle to trust our abilities and expertise. We find ourselves "guilty." We must find our way back to finding ourselves, innocent, worthy and visible. We are too quick to click delete, judge ourselves and discard our value and our original ideas.

We treat our intuition as a “secondhand” make believe skill.

What if you shift the way you think? What if you…

Consider not killing off your original ideas before they see the light of day?

Consider not second guessing your intuition.

Instead, believe there is massive value for other humans and you.

Intuition helps us navigate our human experience. When we are not open to our intuition, it cannot guide us. By allowing the conscious mind (ego/intellect) to be in the driver’s seat, we ignore our intuition.

We pull from intuition and our heart and brain connection to innovate, create, imagine and bring ideas to life. We call on the conscious mind when we need the help of our editor!

Intuition can be an elusive pathway to our heart and brain connection. Unless it isn't!

The heart and brain connection are what regulates our emotions. It helps us make better decisions. When there is a disconnect, we get stuck in-between our emotions.

The language of the subconscious mind is visual. The language of the conscious mind is our intellect (ego).

With this said, it would be quite an ordeal to "think" our way into our intuition.

I developed The Pathfinder Code® *visual discovery techniques* for this reason. To help others speak directly to their subconscious mind. It is only then, that a shift in mindset can take place.

The biggest challenges my clients uncovered and conquered are:

**THE BLOCKS:**

1. Not knowing themselves lacking a deep spiritual connection and self-awareness;
2. Hidden emotional blocks and feeling stuck;
3. Afraid to use their voice, afraid to advocate for themselves in their life and/or business.

**THE SOLUTIONS:**

1. Get to know the parts of yourself that you have avoided looking at, until now. Seek and start a spiritual practice that resonates;
2. Stop treating intuition as a "secondhand" make believe skill.
3. Surrender: do the things that scare you i.e., speaking up, making decisions and taking bold action.

## THE CHANGES YOU WILL EXPERIENCE:

You by choice, can create and live every day as the best version of yourself.

When you surrender and "Energetically Align Your Path with Your Calling".

Yes, this right here is the secret sauce, except it's no secret.

It's a choice and a gift of transformation known as The Pathfinder Code®. In the chapters ahead you will learn more about the visual discovery process.

## MAKE THE CHOICE, EXPERIENCE THE TRANSFORMATION:

- Awaken your personal power
- Find yourself worthy
- Find yourself lovable
- Find yourself innocent

- Find yourself remembering your future (intuition)
- Find yourself advocating for yourself
- You will learn to listen to your own inner voice
- You will silence the noise of what others say about your gifts, talents and ideas.
- You will find yourself more open and flexible
- You will find yourself capable of bringing your original ideas to life rather than killing them off.
- You will find yourself living in the pleasure of life, instead of the pain
- You will find yourself, see and feel your energy and live life on your own extraordinary terms.

**REMEMBER YOUR GIFTS... SO YOU CAN REMEMBER YOUR FUTURE**

# CHAPTER 2:
# STUCK? IT'S TIME TO SHIFT THE ENERGY!

In Chapter One, we discussed the notion of "No more secondhand intuition".

In this chapter we focus on busting through hidden energetic emotional blocks. These blocks take on many forms. They are hard-wired pathways run through your heart/brain connection. These blocks will hold you prisoner and keep you "second guessing" your intuition.

The heart/brain connection or heart coherence is the core of your personal power.

"What is Heart Coherence and Why is it so Powerful? by Janick Leonard is a deep dive into the science behind the heart/brain connection. One statement jumped out at me: "The heart is basically its own brain."

In essence, any emotion experienced in the area of our heart expands. So, love or fear based more of the same lives there for the time you are in that state.

So what emotions are living in the nooks and crannies of your heart space? My first guess is its everything you have avoided until the moment you picked up this book.

Pausing to investigate a nudge, a sign, a message, silences the negative self-talk. This is my "why" for asking this question.

So, I could give you the answer. Pausing is the tool we use to override the marching orders from your "conscious" mind. The Ego part of your personality. This clears the path for your inner wisdom (intuition) and breaks you out of prison and autopilot.

So, how do you shift your energy and align your path with your calling so you can bring your amazing ideas to life?

The transformation I describe happens when choosing a different experience of your emotions. A clear intention is necessary to uncover negative emotions. Some emotions hold an "energetic charge" that keep you stuck when triggered. If these emotions are not released and stay in your heart-space they will continue to cause you grief.

Every transformational coach has tools they use to help others navigate their emotions. One that I have found to be block-busting in my practice, is The Pathfinder Code ® Intuitive Art Reading. This is a creative process I developed that I'll explain later in this book.

Next up, let's talk about energy! Everything in the Universe is energy! Energy is stable and does not change by itself. It is up to you to take the action for a change in your energy to happen.

This is how you start to "energetically align your path with your calling".

***GRAB PAPER AND A PEN FOR WHAT'S UP NEXT!*

## THE 9 STEPS TO THE PROCESS OF CHANGE

The 1st step is **Self-Awareness**. To change something, you must first be aware of it.
The 2nd step is **Willingness**. The real secret to being able to change is the willingness to do so.

The 3rd step is **Understanding**. Write how you believe your circumstances, situations, thoughts, emotions have affected your life.

The 4th step is **Detachment**. Can you see that these thoughts represent only what you learned and experienced? Recognize that they are not part of you and not who you truly are.

The 5th step is **Choice**. Did you have a choice in the situation? If yes, are you accountable to that choice that you made. If you disagree, then you have a choice? If no, then do you have a choice right now to let go and release the past?

The 6th step is **Action**. Take some action today, large or small right now, do something to move toward your new desires.

The 7th step is **Remove Resistance**. What I resist will persist. The harder I try the more difficult it will become. Just let it go.

The 8th step is **Gratitude**. Be grateful for the lessons, the experiences and the opportunity to grow.

The 9th step is **Self-Trust.** This is conveying to yourself that all is well and that you are safe.

When all is well, in your mind, you are living a life that aligns with your desires. It also means you are willing to let go of limiting beliefs. i.e., not good enough, not smart enough, etc.

We were all born with an original intention and ideas that are positive.

If I were to suggest to you that you are here to remember...

That it is your responsibility to *hold the space* for everyone you meet, meaning embracing their dreams, as well as your own. **Would you do it?**

If I suggested to you that the intuitive nudges you have received or receiving now are showing up to awaken you, rather than disrupt you. **Would you believe me?**

A clear intention in these future ways of being is what we are to understand next. We are here to be the catalysts in transforming each other's lives. The anticipated outcome of the transformation is a higher level of functioning on purpose in our life and business settings.

There is a need for a new kind of business ethic, and this is a call to the conscious creators. These are mostly females, influencers, intuitive, empaths, higher sensitive conscious entrepreneurs that are not willing to be silenced or settle. They refuse to ignore and treat their instincts as secondhand intuition.

This conversation is a universal one. It's a practical journey to remembering your future. The former mishandling of the information needed for women to remember who they were born to be, is over. It's time to let your intuition speak to you.

**This book is a guide to *remembering your future* and Rediscovering your Magic.** There are key lessons to remembering your future and bringing your ideas to life. How do you bring your ideas to life?

First, is by not killing them off before they see the light of day.

Second, you need to write them down, honoring the original root thought they evolved from.

Third, you need to look and listen in-between the words that you're actually saying. Think about what your gifts and talents are. Compare this with breathing, does it matter that you miss a breath? Yes, it does.

Everything happens for a reason. I will remind you throughout this book, when talking out loud, listen in between the words. Music would not exist if there was no pause between the notes.

In the chapters ahead, I will be introducing you to the notion of being "talked out of your magic". What magic do I speak of here? It's the magic in-between the time your ideas evolve in your mind to the time you put pen to paper. It is the magic that we were all born to experience.

It's where that magic lives in-between, on that invisible path, that evolves as we do. The invisible path is unique to every human. It exists because we live in a limitless universe.

To make progress on your entrepreneurial path you need to know what you want. Your momentum will be tangible in your words, commitment and bold action. You need to believe in yourself and you need to change your mind, about changing your mind.

You need to do more of what you love and enjoy each day. **Then, you need to actually start doing the "thing" you say you want to do.**

So...

What is it that you want to do?

What are your top three goals?

What have you done so far to actually get what you want?

What has worked for you?

What hasn't worked for you?

Are you asking for help or still trying to do it yourself?

How long have you been wanting whatever it is and living with not having it in your life?

One year, five years, ten years…or more? How many years has it been? Have you lost count? Be honest with yourself. Do the math! Keep this number of years in mind as you journey into the next chapter.

## CHAPTER 3:
## DREAMS ARE RENEWABLE

There are the things that you're good at.

There are things you think you're good at.

There are things that other people say you're good at.

There is one common denominator in these things.

Yep, that would be YOU! Yet, even with all this evidence, you're still not convinced that you are an expert at something!

Then there's the things you might do in your day job. If you have one. You're okay with how you feel about them... you might even be good at these things too.
They get you a paycheck.

Every day, that you are not doing the things that lights you up know these emotions will suck your joy and energy.

This chapter is about calling out to the dreams you want to renew.

These dreams likely include some of those original ideas you killed off and forgot about. It's all good, I had some of these too.

So, someone told you that you couldn't mix and match your superpowers, your ideas, and that they weren't good enough. And you believed what they said.

Here's what I am inviting you to do about this and those forgotten dreams and ideas.

Start thinking about what problem you solve for other people.

Think back to everyone in your life that you've ever spoken with that you've helped in some way. Bring someone to mind, then envision you are sitting across from them and looking into their eyes. What were they asking for your help with?

How did you help them?

How did they feel after you helped them?

How did their life change after you helped them?

How did you feel after hearing from them that you helped them?

Change is a constant on planet Earth. That's one thing that we can count on.

Another one is the pain imprints, made by others during our childhood. These things will continue to trigger us with an emotional charge until we deal with them.

To renew your dreams there are some steps you need to take along the way.

Dreams are not only renewable, they're rebuildable and reclaimable. Dreams do not expire! Another thing about dreams is, they were different when you were a child.

We were all born with an intuitive, creative, gentle, wild and free spirit. Envision yourself as a child, right now. Close your eyes and go back. There is something there that is not with you now.

Do you see it? It's you, the you, before you were talked out of your magic.

It's almost as if… I'm telling you to come up with a formula for making your own magic as an adult.

Really? Yes, but hear me out! Some of us, maybe most of us, were talked out of believing. At some point, it may have even been beaten out of us. Perhaps it was by our parents, teachers…maybe it was school bullies.

In life, in general, most people don't believe in themselves. For this reason, they prefer not to be compared to someone who actually does.

To renew, reboot, reclaim your magic and your dreams, you must be willing to shift. You must be willing to step into the sparkling shoes of that beautiful soul that you were born to be. It was divinely planned, before you took your very first breath.

You've got to find your brave and do it scared! Just make sure you do it!

In the business world, be ready to be compared to someone who does believe in their magic.

**THIS RIGHT HERE IS THE SECRET SAUCE.**

Believing in your magic, believing that what you have to share is worth it and valuable.

**Your heart is where the magic we were all born to experience, lives...that we were somehow talked out of believing!**

## CHAPTER 4:
## WHERE DID YOUR MAGIC GO?

There are words, experiences and life events that have, for a good part of your life, talked you out of your magic. The scary thing is that we at times, talk ourselves out of our magic.

We were not born to be talked out of anything, especially our magic!

It's this and other limiting beliefs, that are imprinted on us, by people we trust, and ourselves, that say, "Tag, you're it."

The point of this chapter is for me to tag you for those things that help you recognize your magic.

**FROM THIS CHAPTER GOING FORWARD**

**I HAVE SOMETHING TO ASK OF YOU... BEFORE YOU START EACH CHAPTER:**

- Close your eyes.

- Take a few deep breaths.
- Then bring into your mind's eye the vision of you being in full appreciation of who you are.
- See yourself smiling.
- Place both your hands over your heart.
- Then bring that self-love and visual into your heart-space and let it linger.
- Take a few more deep breaths
- When you are ready, come back to the room with eyes wide open!

****NEXT, GRAB A PEN AND PAPER!**

You will be starting the journey to see and feel the abundance that is present when you are immersed in your magic.

## YOUR ORIGINAL IDEAS:

1. Make a list of all your original ideas for your business. Every single one of them under the sun!

**My Original Amazing Ideas List:**

---

2. Next, ask your friends, family and those that know you best what they believe you're good at.

Write these down so they are in a list of their own!

Examples:

You are easy to talk to; You are creative; You are a good listener; You are great at building websites and content; You give great advice; You have a knack for design, etc.

**What other people say I am good at?**

---

3. Next, create a list of the things you feel that you are good at! Write down on a list your gifts, talents, super-skills and superpowers.

**What I know for sure I am good at!**

---

4. At this point, you have the three (3) lists I asked you to create.

   a. Your Original Ideas List
   b. What other people say you are good at list
   c. What you know for sure you are good at

5. Next, combine both of the "what you are good at lists" onto one piece of paper. This is your **superpowers "word salad"**. You will be working with the things on this list while reading this book and doing the exercises in here!

**My Superpowers Word Salad**

---

6. Next, pick some words from the "Original Idea List" and some words from the "things you are good at" lists. Here you are matching up the ideas and the words. Do you see the possibilities?

**My Original Ideas and Superpowers Word Salad**

___

Be sure when you make this list, they are the words and ideas that resonate the most with you. These words will make you smile from ear to ear! They feel like "home".

7. Next, get a clean piece of paper and write down "one" idea from your original idea list!

**My #1 Original Idea**

___

8. Next, choose four (4) words from the Word Salad list in Step 5.

**My Core Values:**

______________________________________________

These four words are your CORE VALUES. In your business, everything you do and say must align with these four values. They are the heart of your branding.

9. Next, we are exploring your branding color palette. Then, make a list of your favorite colors.

**My Core Super Colors**

______________________________________________

I love using Canva to create graphics. I found a great article to share on color theory that you can read to help you select your branding colors:

https://www.canva.com/learn/color-meaningssymbolism/.

You can also Google the words "color meaning and symbolism." There are limitless ways to educate yourself on what each color means. You will want to read up and research the colors and know why you select them. Each one of them is part of you energetically aligning your path with your calling. We are creating and nurturing the fresh ideas and vibration of your branding!

In the article *"Color Psychology: Does It Affect How You Feel?"* the authors Kendra Cherry (and Steven Gans, M.D., who did the medical review) share, "Color is a powerful communication tool and can be used to signal action, influence mood, and even influence physiological reactions." You can read at https://www.verywellmind.com/color-psychology2795824

Why is this exercise so important? It's to help you develop your intuitive investigative skills that you need to do your inner work and mesh them with the colors that speak to you.

It's important to know which colors resonate with you and their meaning. This is so you surround yourself with the energy that lifts you up. This is about knowing yourself on a deeper level and understanding what you need.

Think back to your first time you colored! This is a milestone in every child's life and to be celebrated.

Why? It was the birthday of little "you" meshing your natural knowing (intuition) with your creativity. No instructions were given or needed. Even if they were you wouldn't have listened anyway. I know I didn't!

Little humans always color outside the lines. Big humans should always color outside the lines. It's my belief that there are no lines and never have been!

This exercise is to mesh out who you are and what you are awesome at. Then mix it with the words and colors that best represent the real you. The one that is ready to rediscover your magic and bring your own ideas to life.

Note: This YOU is the one that refuses to partake in building someone else's dreams. Entrepreneurs build their own dreams first, so they then help other people.

This exercise was designed to cut a wedge through the mind chatter and the self-doubt. It is an invitation to you. One that I hope you take me up on. I wrote this book for you. While you may not believe that any of this is possible. I know you will when you have read this book in its entirety. My goal in this chapter was to give you some tools to start creating and meshing your ideas and superpowers. Some people when asked, say they do not know what they are good at. You know what your magic is. You simply need to claim it, believe it and live it. Then use your voice to deliver the message.

In the chapters ahead, we are going to use the lists you made here to create the "voice" and message for your business!

Have fun with these exercises – we are mining for your hidden gold!

**Remember, dreams are renewable, rebootable and reclaimable and have no expiration date!**

# CHAPTER 5: THE PATHFINDER CODE® POWER PRACTICES

In this book we weave in the physical, emotional and spiritual aspects to lead you to the path to rediscover your magic. Your whole person requires you to learn to take care of your body, become grounded so that every step of the way on your personal growth and entrepreneurial journey is sustainable. While this is not a comprehensive list by any means, I share these, my own power practices, that have helped me remember what I need, when I need them and why I need them.

## WHAT WE EXPERIENCE, WE REMEMBER.

This part of the book will focus on using your voice, moving and taking care of your body and creating the environment you need to get a simple energetic tune-up anytime you want to tap into these resources.

## POWER PRACTICES FOR ENERGETIC ALIGNMENT

**Breathwork**: Develop breath awareness. There is a close connection between the pattern of our breathing and our state of mind. Develop breathing in and out in a more relaxed state, taking your time to experience this.

***Lengthen your breath*** with each set of inhaling and exhaling three times, taking the time to slowly navigate your experience.

***Deepen your breath*** with each set of three. To help you with this process, visualize it as energy, a light, flowing down into your abdomen area and out again. Do this three times in and out, and with each breath.

***Practice loud sighs, ohms with your breathing*** to warm up your body, develop inner strength and will power. Inhale deeply and slowly then exhale with a vibration, a sound using your voice and breath. Do this in a set of three. Whatever feels good to you. If you like to sing, do it after your vibrational breathing exercise!

***Singing*** brings about happy feelings and is known for the empowerment and good vibes it brings when you sing along to your favorite songs.

***Mesh your intuition and creativity with your breathwork.*** Gather up a few items: a straw, some watercolor paper and a watercolor palette. Put on some music, grab your favorite drink. Dip your brush into a cup of water, then your paint palette, then place droplets onto the paper. Next take your straw and use your breath to move the droplets naturally to see where the movement takes them! Keep creating until the artwork no longer calls to you. Take a moment to be with your creation and see what there is for you to understand about it and yourself. Get a small frame and place your artwork somewhere, that you can see it every day. It will remind you of your experience. Most people find they want to do more of this.

**Grounding yourself**: You can do this by talking a walk or practice "Earthing". This is a therapeutic technique that involves doing activities that "ground" or electrically connect you to the earth. This practice relies on earthing science and grounding physics to explain how the electrical charges from the earth can have positive effects on your body. This means taking a walk to the local park or beach, taking off your shoes and spend time with your bare feet touching the grass or sinking into the sand and water. You can find out more about this practice by simply doing online research. There are lots of positive benefits. I personally do it daily and it feels wonderful!

**Hydrate:** While everyone is different, I personally strive for a gallon of water per day. Now this is not for everyone. Drink the amount that works for you. Just be sure to drink! If you are thirsty, chances are you are dehydrated. So use that as a sign to drink up! Your body will thank and reward you!

**Eat Organic:** While they are a bit more expensive, organic foods are generally free of contaminants that damage health. They also tend to be enriched in immune boosting nutrients because of how they were grown. A healthy diet is key to having the energy to do your inner work!

**Cook a Meal with Love:** Cooking is creative and gives us the opportunity to experience peaceful and happy thoughts while preparing a meal. I love to listen to Andres Bocelli when I cook! When you eat the meal prepared with this loving feeling, it easily becomes a celebration of breaking bread, enjoying life and it nurtures our spirit. Yes, we eat to refuel and have energy, but this practice can make meal prep something to really look forward to.

**Exercise:** Whatever you are physically able to do. Take a walk, get some sunshine. Dance, wiggle, just keep moving your body!

**Pamper yourself:** Take long showers and baths. Turn off the lights and light a candle. Soak your feet in foot spa at home with some scented Epsom salts, lavender and mint is my favorite!

**Sleep:** Use sleep as an energetic tool to empower yourself in every aspect of your wellbeing. Getting enough sleep can make or break your creativity. You will thrive and feel far more grounded when you get sufficient sleep. Yes, in this book I talk about being extreme for a "season". Knowing when to intuitively take a break is key to thriving in business and at home. It will foster positive relationships and more communication. Plus, you will be fresh and feel ready to take on any challenge!

**Your Home and Office:** In Chapter 4, we covered your Core Colors. Take the colors you found that resonated with you the most and surround yourself with them in all of your living spaces. Clear out your space and declutter! Be sure to open windows and let the sunlight in often. Candles, pillows and lots of throw blankets make for a cozy and ambient living space. Decorate your office with symbolic things that make you smile. Plants, especially lucky bamboos and money trees are a fun way to bring the outdoors, inside!

**Create a vision board and crystal altar:** Vision boards are created using words and images from magazines. The vision board is representative of the things you are building in your life and business they are a daily reminder to live "as if" it's all already happened. Believe that it has.

Some get crystal chips and place them on a canvas and incorporate them into a painting! Crystals are a playful way to surround yourself with more of the colors and tangible items that ground you spiritually and energetically. It's also fun to research the origin and meaning of each crystal and place them according to what you feel you need. I have crystal quartz, amethyst and apatite placed on my laptop so they are always in my view while working.

**Your People:** Surround yourself with those that encourage and support you. It's important to have both a support system for your life and business. You will recognize your people. They are your top fans! More on this in the chapters ahead.

# CHAPTER 6:
# CREATING THE VISION

Look at the world now, through your own eyes, for the first time in a very long time. It's your turn. It's your time to set some goals. It's your time to make a decision, commit and take action on the work you did in Chapter 4!

The path to renew those dreams and bring them and to life, means:

1. Listening to your voice in your own words and starting to speak up, out loud.

2. You are being called to advocate for yourself, with yourself.

Stay with me! So, you don't push back on the momentum you have at this very moment. Know this is not a typo. You heard me right. You must advocate for yourself, with yourself.

Because guess what? Out of all the negativity you might have experienced in your lifetime... what you have told yourself, was the catalyst for you to believe, for even a nano-second that your magic was gone.

You see, it's just not "possible" for your magic to be gone.

You were born with it and it was gifted to you before you took your very first breath!

In the earlier chapter, you gathered up your "word salad" to come up with your core values and colors. So now it's time to be super mindful.

In the chapters ahead, you will be creating several things for your business.

Whether you have one you want to reboot, reclaim, redesign or you have a new vision that you want to get started on.

I see you, and want to remind you, that you are architect of what gets to be in the room of your life!

**SEE YOURSELF "AS IF" YOU ARE THERE!**

How does one do this? To start, there is your inner voice or critic, it either helps you make decisions and take action, or it stalls you. It's that old adage about getting in your own way or stepping out of your own way.

Here's the thing- you've got to picture yourself in the situations you desire to be in.

I will take the example of some of my clients' aspirations. Some want to be a life coach, head up a wellness hub, some full-time artists, etc.

What they all have in common is they are yearning to get to know themselves better. To do this they have to understand which voice they are listening to. Their inner voice or the inner critic.

The goal is to steer clear of the inner critic so they can achieve the desired results.

To get into the groove of bringing your ideas to life, who you will serve, take a moment to reflect on what this looks like. This is the why behind the exercises in the earlier chapters.

***GRAB YOUR PAPER AND PEN AND ANSWER THESE QUESTIONS.**

You will need this for the exercises in future chapters.

1. **Elevator Pitch:** Who you are, who you serve and the results you help them get.

Example: I help female entrepreneurs clear emotional blocks, find their voice, energetically align their path and calling, so they can bring their ideas to life.

2. The **Vision** for your business-what will you be known for?

3. The **Mission Statement** for your business-What you do and how you do it?

4. Your **Unique Selling Proposition**- What makes you unique? What do you do differently from other businesses in your genre?

5. **Your ICA (Ideal Client Avatar) Story**. This is a fictional character who embodies your best client

profile. The information and data should be based in reality.

Here are some examples of questions you would ask to create your ICA's story. The example I give are questions to identify a female ICA looking for a life coach.

Women AGES (i.e., 38 to 58 years old)

Ethnicity (background and country of origin)

Where has she lived most of her life?

Where has she visited?

Does she have children?

What is her occupation? What is her financial status?

What does she want? Career transition? Start a business?

Has she taken personal growth courses or hired a coach?

Where does she hang out online?

Do your own research. Google "Ideal Client Avatar". Add other questions that come to mind and those you compile through online research. Note: This is by no means a comprehensive list of questions to identify your ICA. This is something I help my clients with. This section is to introduce the ICA concept to you.

This data you compile in this exercise will assist you to later identify your niche and target markets.

6. **Practice: If it's Not on Your Calendar it Will Not Happen!**

Whatever you may want to do, you have to start testing the waters! Set a date with someone that is going to help you practice your elevator pitch and presentation. With most businesses being online now, setting up a video conference with an app like Zoom works best.

Get a planner or online calendar platform. I recommend Calendly. To be successful you need to prepare, be consistent, practice and never give up.

Enter all appointments, even your practice sessions with a friend or colleague. If you don't it will not happen or you might forget about it.

If you do not have anyone to practice with you can create a post. The post can be on Facebook or another platform where you believe your ICA hangs out. It should read something like this:

**Example Market Research Social Media Post:**

"Hello Friends: I am doing some market research and want to interview women that want to launching a life coach business. In exchange, I'd like to give you a 30- minute marketing strategy session for your next event."

You can add in your own details about exactly who you are looking to interview.

*Give them some value of whatever service you are offering.

For example, I was about to do a live event and a marketing coach did a post like the one I am describing. I did the interview to answer the questions for her research and in exchange she helped me with a marketing plan for my event!

So, starting out you may be able to exchange services with another professional in your genre. This interviewing process of connecting face to face with a potential ideal client is how you find your first "why" you want to do what you do. I was an ideal client for this marketing professional.

You need to know your why and get some insight into what the demand is for the problems that you can solve with your skill sets.

This is where that "word salad" you prepared comes in. You need to know what you are good at and the problems you solve for people. This is the path to bring your ideas to life!

## IF IT'S NOT ON YOUR CALENDAR IT IS NOT GOING TO HAPPEN

# CHAPTER 7: UNSCRIPTED

Give yourself at least one year to integrate your new side hustle or full-time business into your life. It may take you another year or two to be able to leave your day job. I am speaking from experience here. Be sure to have at least 6 months or more of your monthly expenses in the bank. There are lots of other things you will need to do for your business. This chapter is to give you an overview of some of the things that I had to learn when launching my business.

My goal in this book is to help find your way, your voice, and be your own advocate in your life and business so you can live life on your own terms, unscripted. I say "unscripted" because of the work we are doing in the exercises. Once you know who you are, what your message is, who you help, and the results they experience, from working with you ... you will find and know what feels like "home" to you. I call this your "home frequency," where the words just come to you from your heart and there is no script needed

I use a small note with a list of prompts to keep me on track when speaking. I have done the exercises I am sharing in this book. I only teach and speak on the things I am passionate about and have expert knowledge of. While I am always learning to expand my knowledge base, it is important to stay on brand and message.

An example of this is you hear a competitor teaching on topics that are trending that you know are outside his/her expertise. Rock steady in your own lane! Because a topic is trending it doesn't mean you have to jump on board and become an expert in it.

Speak and teach on those things you have a deep understanding and knowledge base. Yes!
Continuing education and expanding your reach is great! By all means, you must continue to grow. Research before speaking on topics that are not relevant to your genre or core values. If they interest you, reflect on how they are relevant and what problem it solves for your ICA.

Now I am not saying, "Do not experiment!" We must take risks to grow! If I told you I was going to also teach you how to do your taxes in this book you might not take my other content seriously. Why? This book is not about teaching you to do your taxes.

I am sure you get the big picture of what I am relaying here.

This is how to become "unscripted". Knowing your voice, your message and your expertise inside out, upside down. The goal here is to wean yourself off the stack of paper! After you complete the exercises in this book, it is my vision that you too can become unscripted! I know the ropes here...this was my biggest challenge!

Think about the promise you are making to your clients. Think about the promise you are keeping.

This is where your magic lives, stay on brand and message and practice! This is how to develop this forward thinking to make becoming unscripted a reality. This is the path to energetically aligning your path with your calling.

**What becoming "unscripted" means:**

You know who you are and have the ability to use your voice to convey your message and story from your heart space, without looking at a script.

# CHAPTER 8: BELIEVING IN YOUR MAGIC

In the last chapter I suggested you get some practice on your pitch or presentation. If you want other people to believe in your magic, meaning, your ideal clients, you need to believe in it!

Those people that believe in you is the source of the "social proof" you will gather. This social proof comes in the form of reviews and recommendations.

You can start asking for these, once you are out there doing the thing you say you want to do! So, whether its practicing with a friend or a client. If you want social proof you need to take action! You cannot collect a review on a session you didn't have or a product you didn't sell.

Another recommendation: Hold a local in -person or online event. It could be anything under the sun that relates to what you do. This is especially true when you are planning to launch your business.

Give yourself this experience. It is a gift because it pushes you to "lose" the paperwork and be a self-sustaining magical unit.

**Stepping into the shoes of your unscripted self:**

1. It helps you test out your understanding of your branding
2. It will help you experience your cognitive recognition of your content.
3. It will give you measurable results:

That will either work in your favor or not because of how you articulated your message. Or the results will let you know you need more practice. You can then practice more to develop a better way to articulate your message.

This is more for your growth. This is why a message from your heart is always on brand.

The experience of interacting with you, unscripted, is your opportunity to shine.

Use the hesitation you may feel to fuel your desire to excel at this. See yourself having done it, many times. Feel your growth as both you and your vision mature and align. You are divinely supported.

You cannot teach someone to be heart-centered. You are the only one that can deliver your message.

Are you in a business where you plan to train a team or a virtual assistant?

How can you do this if you do not know your message yourself?

How will anyone else believe in your magic if you don't believe in it?

There are things in life that are constant companions to us, one being our emotions and how we see ourselves.

There are people that will support and love you in your journey. But there is only one person's opinion that matters.

Yes, that would be YOU!

You need your own support, self-love, self-trust.

You need to embrace your inner wisdom.

You need to be your own cheerleader, and you need to feed whatever you're hungry for.

You may be one of those people that never stops, even if it exhausts you at times.

Getting to know and understand why you're wired to do what you do is really important. So, keep testing the waters with each one of your core values.

How can you expand how you serve others?

There was greatness assigned to you before you took your first breath. Maybe you found this out early in life!

This greatness is the spark that ignites the creativity within you, and in your future self.

There are going to be people that hand you things to remind you of who you are.

One of those people was my sister, where she knew from our childhood, that we were both meant to build our own dreams. Not stay stuck in day jobs building someone else's dream. Yes, there are day jobs that will simultaneously pay the bills and steal your joy.

The thing is you must be self-aware and consistent so that your magic does not escape into the ether, permanently.

Remember the girl I talked about at the beginning of the book? That girl was me. This is why I can sense when another human has been talked out of their magic. It's both a blessing and a curse. It also depends on what one does with the burden of this knowledge, and which way it goes.

What I did, I surrendered to the notion of believing that I was meant for, far more than a day job. I accepted the notion that I had to energetically align with who I was born to be. I had to stop denying myself this honor.

**I HAD TO HOLD THE SPACE FOR MYSELF, TO JUST BE ME.**

I want for you, what I want for me. Everything I share in this chapter; I want you to start doing. Do not stop until you have hit pay dirt and your "home" frequency.

One more thing, Yes, there was a best friend named Susan and everything I shared about her is true. The thing is, she was me, and I was her.

**THIS IS EVERY WOMAN'S STORY THAT HAS EVER STOPPED BELIEVING IN HERSELF AND HER MAGIC!**

There are people that have seen your greatness and your ability to help others. These are the people you need to surround yourself with.

Part of your responsibility to keep your magic alive is surrounding yourself with the people that believe in you. These people are your people. They are your biggest fans; they love and support you even on the days where you do not feel capable of doing it. Find your people. You will need them and they will need you. One more thing about these people, you can never, ever, have too many of them!

**It is my hope that you understand the underlying message in this chapter.**

## HAVE YOU REALIZED BY NOW THAT YOUR MAGIC STARTS WITH YOU?

Just show up and do what you do, and so will the ideal clients that need your help. Start rooting for yourself. If you were stranded somewhere, would you drive 100 miles to go pick yourself up?

Logistically this doesn't make sense. It does not need to. It is more about you paying attention and listening to your own voice. It is to make certain you are not quitting or defaulting back to where you were before you picked up this book.

It's about taking the next step and doing what you need to do to help yourself not only rediscover your magic, but to unleash it! Why? So you can have the life you want and live it on your own terms.

Of course, you love others, but you need to love yourself even more. You need to learn to be creative in how you advocate for yourself, with yourself.

Find acceptance in who you aspire to be. Then be the best version of yourself every day. Comparing yourself, only to who you were the day before, if you are compelled to compare. Your goal is to live out the vision you have for yourself.

Who are you?

Are you the creative, unscripted, intuitive soul with a mystical quest that came to planet Earth with a purpose? Yes, you are!

There is only one thing left to do. Get moving and start playing "all in", you are on a mission to Rediscover Your Magic! This is not a time to shrink or play small!

These creative energies and drive cannot be prescribed, you are born with them. You cannot lose them. You cannot shake them off. They're always there.

This is where the struggle exists. Because we fight with ourselves, and we fight with the "invisibles".

**THESE ARE THE HIDDEN BLOCKS, THE THINGS THAT ARE UNDONE, THAT NUDGE YOU, HAUNT YOU AND KEEP YOU UP AT NIGHT.**

In the chapter ahead I will teach you how to fill your life with the colors that light you up so those hidden blocks can be seen and dealt with.

# CHAPTER 9:
# THE INVISIBLES

What are the invisibles? To me, it's that energy in between the words. It's the tasks, our TO DO list in our life and business that we cannot see because they are NOT DONE.

They are the perpetually UNDONE things. The energy of the UNDONE is what runs interference with our being aligned with our purpose and path.

I mentioned earlier in this book that music is made because there are pauses between the notes. It's the same thing with energetically aligning your path with your calling. Part of this means paying attention to the colors you surround yourself with. Pay attention to the words you say about yourself. Pay attention to all the things that you have believed over the years. Notice some no longer serve you. These are the ones that it's time to let go of, to turn off.

You can see the "invisible" path if you look closely enough. It is the place you go to when you quiet yourself, the place where all of your thoughts have free reign in your mind. The invisibles reside in a duality, this is where the danger is energetically.

There is somewhat of a Ying and Yang to the invisible path, it's your safe place, but also where the conscious mind (ego) can creep in with some of the old paradigm language of negative self-talk.

It is daunting and can be physically exhausting to deal with the invisibles. But here's the thing, once you know how to foster a deep connection with yourself, learn how to deal with both light and shadow energy, there won't be any myth you cannot bust through.

Part of your creative toolkit is the aligning your energy with your core colors. It's also to use those color to help you seen the invisibles, the UNDONE things that stall your progress.

To do this, grab the lists you created from the exercises you did in Chapters 4 and 5. This will help you map out a vibrant 12-month plan with a clear intention.

## THE NEXT RIGHT PATH – 12 MONTH PLAN

**Grab paper and a pen or type if that is your preference!**

1. **Read and learn new things to maintain your edge and knowledge base.** Make a list of the things that help you stay true to you. Read books on these topics, that are related to the thing you want to do, authored by the people doing it already. Tie in one of your core colors to see where it leads you in this exercise. Maybe you are looking for books that have a blue cover if that is one of your core colors.

2. F**ocus!** Every minute that you are not working in your day job, if you have one, or taking care of yourself and your family, I invite you to envision and start documenting the services or products you want to provide to other people. Make a list

of all that comes to mind. You may have made some notes from the exercises in the earlier chapters.

3. **Research** to identify and interview your ideal clients to develop the insight you need. I provided a Marketing Research Social Media post in an earlier chapter. You will bring value while exchanging your services.

4. **Social proof from market research interviews:** The only way that we can truly help another human is to bring them value. Should this be for free, initially at first, that is reasonable. It is a quick way to get social proof (reviews) and digital assets (video testimony) that you can use on social media. You would be amazed at how many people would be absolutely delighted at the value that you're going to bring them. Do not underestimate the impact that you can make in someone's life. Tie in one or more of your core colors with your social media posts.

In this chapter, I am meshing the notion of your core colors with your content so you can have a visual in your mind's eye. It's also to keep you on brand and message.

**5. Who do you need to help you level up from?**

**Where you are right now as you read this book?**

**What alternatives are there to save money?**

Identifying your next right path and mapping out a plan includes, seeking out the people that will help you accomplish your goals. This will change so be flexible and give yourself grace. Keep in mind that the people you interviewed might be a good resource for bartering or exchanging services.

**Do you have a planner or notebook?** If not get one that leaves you room for lots of notes and client profiles. If it doesn't exist create one. I once created a client planner with a 3-ring binder! It was better than anything I found online.

**Tame your to do list:** Trello is a great tool for this.

**Content and Design:** Learn to use Canva.

**Professional Photos:** You can take great pro-selfies with a few attempts!

**Stylist:** Check out Pinterest for some fresh ideas on dressing for the role you play in your business. There are also college students studying design that need hours. If you can swing it, there are professional styling companies out there or just Google what you need online!

**Admin Tasks:** Complete admin tasks yourself as much as is possible in the beginning. Or, exchange services with another professional.

As you make your way on this journey you will know when it's time to take the next step up to hire admin help or a virtual assistant.

The one investment I did not skimp on was hiring several experienced coaches that truly cared about my success.

Yes, the "do it all herself" magic tool kit had all my gifts and talents in it! But I quickly learned to take inventory of my tools and saw how essential this step up was to my momentum when starting out!

## CHAPTER 10:
## MAKE BELIEVE, MADE TANGIBLE

This chapter lays out the groundwork for those of you looking to exit jobs that make you sick and tired, steal your joy and your dreams.

**Before we dive in…remember to PRACTICE GRATITUDE for the financial support that job has given you!**

How and where have you spent most of your working life?

Have you been building someone else's dreams or your own?

**Next, I have a story to share with you!**

This is story about a real person, but for this hero's journey, we will call her Nicole. Nicole is a Director and supervises a staff of 25 employees at a company in Northern Washington. She has been with the company for 15 years and is one of the founding employees of this corporation. She is lives in Redmond, Washington, a suburb near Seattle.

She shares her home with her husband, John and Pomeranian pup named "Poppy". She drives a BMW sedan as she no longer needs the large SUV she did while raising her children. She grew up in Seattle and attended the University there. It kept her close to her family and while her children were transitioning into their own lives. She majored in Business English because of her love of writing and reading as a child.

She also has a creative side hustle for extra income and socializing. She uses this income to buy supplies for her organic wildflower skin care products. She creates and sells her products at local farmers' markets.

She is over working for a corporation selling their products. She wants to branch out and learn how to sell kits and teach her process of making organic products. Her nights and weekends ... are filled with formulating oils/herbs for her organic products. She attends whole life events. She also collects crystals and gems, anything, connected with spirituality and higher self.

She has received big kudos at work for helping with the corporate "spirit day" activities. This permits her to show up for a short time as her alter ego creative energized self.

While she cares about the state of the world, she does not care to join the debate. She is passionate about the environment and clean living. She "secretly" cheers on those who advocate for humanitarian causes. She is quiet about her true feelings here and in most of her relationships.

Her spouse John works in financial industry and has been with the same company for 20 years. He is usually supportive, he can at times question her "why" at times making it more about his needs. He knows she has been researching her "exit plan" from her job for a very long time. He also knows she has been looking for the plan and coach whose cadence is in alignment with her vision. He is somewhat hot and cold about her building her dreams. This is another dilemma she contends with daily.

About her dreams, what were they anyway? She had a passion for creating clean organic skin care products. She wanted people to have the option to use toxic free products. Especially people like her mother with a chronic illness like breast cancer. She has toyed with the idea of taking her products into natural foods market. She envisioned talking to their buyers in her mind's eye. She reflects often on what it would feel like to sell her products somewhere other than the farmer's market. She has kept this to herself as its part of the "secret life" she has desired for years.

She enjoys nature, flowers, looking up each flower's story. From this, she learns how to use them in her products, oils and teas. She frequents the learning labs at the local colleges to learn as much as she can about organics.

Nicole is spiritual and loves all things connected with nature. She would love to sell her products and teach others how to make their own products. She had an idea to sell kits for this.

She is sometimes introverted. But snaps out of it once she has tried the new experience she has been contemplating.

She does not like most things on TV or anything that has heavy or negative undertones. She is good with a comedy or fantasy story. She has enough inner battles to contend with and does her best to know where to draw the line.

Friends tell her that she is creative, good at organizing and making people feel special. Yet, these same friends, tell her the small amount she makes at the farmers market is a waste of time. This goes a long way to reinforce her lack of confidence, courage and negative self-talk.

When I met Nicole, she was sick and tired. She was at a place in her life that she no longer wants to live a life, unfulfilled. She worried that if she didn't act soon, the years would pass her by.

At our first meeting, she shared that a woman she supervised was leaving the company. To launch her own business. This news caused her to default to her negative self-talk and emotional eating. She admitted to comforting herself by watching "Eat, Pray and Love" for the 3rd time. All while gobbling down two pints of Ben & Jerry's. Much like the actress in the movie, she was at a turning point in her life. One where she wanted to embark on "her" journey. The one that had been on perpetual "replay" in her mind's eye for years. She sighed while sharing her backstory with me. She let out a big exhale when she said "I have lost count of the years it seems."

She was exhausted from safeguarding her "secret". She was sick and tired of being online at night and looking at the "how to" e-books that live in the safe realm of her laptop. She often thought to herself "who did she think she was to dabble in this playground?" She knew she had to do something, her thoughts, her life and the time that passed were out of control!

Her frustration has fueled her desires into a decision. In our meeting she shared that she could not stand another minute in the masquerade! While she was afraid to be the center of attention. She was finally serious and no longer playing around.

The days and months that followed came and went. So did her decision making. Stalled month after month. It took an onslaught of physical symptoms that made her ill to speak up, decide, commit and take action. She shared that the energy she felt was so heavy that it was suffocating her. She developed physical symptoms. Co-workers had noticed that she was sighing very loud and asked if she was alright.

After hearing some of her story, I surmised that she had never used her voice in this manner to speak up for herself. What also surfaced was that her husband was a narcissist and made her life miserable.

So, what exactly did Nicole need from me? Was it just a way to bring her ideas for her business to life? No, it was far more.

She needed some to keep her accountable.

She needed to find herself worthy and innocent.

She needed to face her self-imposed prison. She needed to advocate for herself at work, in life and to make her side hustle be more than a pipe dream.

She also needed game plan on how to work on her side hustle while working.

She needed a mindset shift on how to deal with setbacks.

After many months of coaching, healing and planning. Step by step. Nicole was able to put a plan in place to calendar her exit date from her job. Yes, she had finally made the decision, she committed. But now, she still needed to speak up and act on the plan to make her exit a from her job a reality.

**If it's not on your calendar it isn't going to happen!**

## HITTING A WALL

When you start to sift through new possibilities, like Nicole did, some ugly stuff is likely to come up. Expect the unexpected. The relationships you find yourself in now are ones you allowed, whether good or not so good. There were unspoken words and invisible soul contracts with fine print you agreed too. You are now realizing that you have found the bravery to speak up and step up.

About that fine print. Was it not legible? Was it in a language that you could not understand? Guess what? It's not your fault. Any person, that who has energetically aligned their path. With their calling, would not be able to interpret this fine print. The lens of clarity is the interpreter.

That ugly stuff is the "dis-ease" that has made women like Nicole and thousands of others hit a wall in their exit plan. The uneasiness, the symptoms, the perpetual questions became the chronic pain. The "disease" and the silence that has plagued, women for far too long.

Advocating for yourself with your voice is by far the biggest catalyst on the planet. It is the trigger that determines whether your magic is at risk or ready to ignite the spark within.

## THE EXIT PLAN: Decide, Commit and Take Action!

1. Decide what you want so you know what it is. Be very specific. (i.e., exit your day job, career change, walk away from a particular relationship in your life or business, improve your health, etc.)

2. Decide who gets to be in the room of your new life you are building. Not everyone gets to stay. This isn't saying you won't have a relationship with them, you may decide it best that they not be privy to the inner workings of your exit plan. Avoid negative people who do not support you, they are a dealbreaker for your success. You can be friends with them again when you have reached your goals, if you feel it will be a healthy decision at the time.

3. Decide and adapt your daily routine to include the practice of self-
care. See yourself in that place now and appreciate the way the changes make you feel.

4. Interview professionals that will be part of your dream team of support. This would include a coach or mentor.

5. Decide how you will navigate the relationships you have at work and home. There will need to be a heart to heart discussion of your exit plan. This is where you pull out all the stops and level up how you are using your voice.

6. Reflect on the "work-arounds" that you have used in your lifetime. Recall those insights. Those are part of your original ideas. You will need those so do not kill them off. Be sure you have a running list of these treasures because you're going to use them later when we mesh it all together.

7. Now it is time to learn how to release the heavy energy that is lingering. This means you will need to get help to uncover your hidden emotional blocks so you are not blindsided as you continue with your exit plan.

8. The ultimate goal of this book is to show you the way, to Energetically Align your Path with your Calling. For you to be so comfortable in your own skin when you use your voice, you no longer need the paper as a guide. Metaphorically it's the day job that is the source of all the "paper". It's the paper that silences your voice.

9. Intuition, Creativity, and Imagination will become your constant companions now. They are required as part of the exit plan. It's how you will hold the space; they are the container for your energy, your vision, and retaining your magic on this journey of alignment. You see, there will be days when you don't have the wherewithal to do it for yourself. So, part of the pulling and pushing what you think is "make believe" is actually the most tangible and high value of all your skills.

## OWNING YOUR POWER:

The goal here is to better understand how the world you came from, when you decided to speak up, will affect what the world will look like through your eyes today and tomorrow.

As you're reading this book, I want you to think about when you're owning your personal power and when you're giving it away. It's the times where you're comparing yourself to other people that you're giving your power away.

There are many voices present in your life. **One of them is yours**. Many voices will have opinions. The only part of those voices I want you to listen to are the ones that unconditionally love and support you.

The other voices have no place in making your magic or personal power tangible. The bigger goal here is to identify, accept, and walk through the hidden blocks that show up time and again.

This is what energetically aligning your path with your calling looks like and feels like. There is a process of change that has to take place.

The change created in the processes described in this book include deep inner work. They will challenge you and fulfill you simultaneously.

What are the things that you need to work through to go from make believe to made tangible?

**Grab some paper and a pen and make some notes before heading into the next chapter.**

If you resonate with Nicole. Let this be the beginning of rewriting your story and that soul contract!

# CHAPTER 11:
# IMAGINATION, INFLUENCE & INTUITION

IMAGINATION gives people something they did not know they were missing.

INFLUENCE is the persuasive power that a person or event has over you.

INTUITION is the ability to understand something immediately; a thing that one knows or considers likely from instinctive feeling rather than conscious reasoning.

These virtues have a common theme. They invite you into the energy that exists outside of your conscious mind. In-between the words, images and emotions.

If only, we could bottle this up and use it to shake off any residual "not enough-ness" so it could never rent space, in our minds again. Ever.

There are people in your life that you are going to learn many lessons from. From my father, I learned to fight and acceptance of the things I could not change. I was the one person by his side as he prepared to leave the planet and his earthly human form. He was the one that showed me who I was destined to be. He saw things in me most of which he knew could not be contained. The wild child that was always in trouble in her teens, but the one that made him laugh the hardest. He saw into me, just like I see into the you who is reading this book. This right here, is more of the WHY for writing this book.

I don't talk about my mother much. The reason it's so relevant in this chapter is the influence that both she and my father had on me. My mother was bipolar and manic. When her mental state was under control through medication, she cooked a lot. Being from an Italian family growing up in the Bronx, hers hailing from Southern Italy. I remember her handing out cookies to my friends when they came calling. This is a vivid flashback for my six-year old self. In these moments when she was stable and not flipping tables while we were eating dinner, she was this woman I call "the cookie giver".

All of this showed up in my life every day that she was in it. She was extracted from my life at age seven after several mental breakdowns and episodes brought on by her mental state.

I did not see my mother again until 1999 on a trip to New York with my sister. A question comes up for me while writing this. Was there ever a time where she was checked in? Why does it matter now? It just does. Because of the influence on my self-worth. Yes, she was checked in. In those "cookie giver" moments of time. There are no other memories in my childhood where she appeared to be a normal loving mother.

**Becoming a mother and the woman I did not have growing up was my path to healing.**

So, how does this pertain to influence? Because I realized there is much I blocked out. Remnants of childhood scars that were imprinted on me. They would come in flashbacks at unexpected times. Why those, why then, why now?

Depending on your life experience there may be things that you've blocked out that are still imprinted on you.

I'm sharing this with you because talking out loud might trigger something in you and one of your core memories. I underwent deep spiritual and emotional discovery work to remove the imprints. I am so glad I did.

See yourself starting to heal. See and feel having influence over your own life and discarding the imprints. Imagine yourself, not being at the mercy of a parent, a companion, a boss, or a bully from your childhood. There are also adult bullies too that I will warn you about.

Imagine yourself as your younger self, but knowing better. Imagine in your mind's eye your future self, knowing more. That no matter what you've blocked out, no matter what has happened, you do know better and know more.

The lessons in the earlier chapters dealt with how to energetically align your path with your calling, deal with the things you are afraid to do. The most important one... how to use your voice to support yourself while doing them.

No script needed, just you and your voice. It is required of you at this moment. If you cannot show up for yourself, with your voice, it is a deal breaker. Should you choose to not take your turn, and carve out this time for you, those new paths will linger in the distant future, that is, until they don't.

You see, when we block out past hurts, we silence ourselves. We surrender to being talked out of our magic. We forget who we are and what we came here to do. The personalities and people that undermine your well-being and momentum will appear in your lifetime, time and again.

Until, you do the inner work, so you can recognize the arrival of the misinformation. Listen to your heart, your intuition and imagine yourself stronger than the past, present or future influences that might trigger you getting stuck again.

This is the question I have for you. Why don't you talk about the person or situation that brings you grief? I ask, because you likely need to, just as I needed to, and you need to forgive them as well as forgive yourself.

GUILT is not a productive emotion. So, while this is a glimpse into bits and pieces of my story, it might be someone else's too that needs to read this. It has been the story of many of my clients. The story just has different names, places, people and emotions. It's a story that needs to be told for healing and energetic alignment to take place. It's a story that shines a light on how childhood influences can and do affect one's ability to use their imagination.

Recall the story at the beginning of this book about Susan. The truth is…I am Susan, and parts of this story could be similar to yours.

You see, when you start to take charge of what you allow to influence your life, you will start to see the things that are good for you.

About a year ago I attended a gathering. There I met a woman who asked me why I didn't talk to or about my mother.

What? A complete stranger asking me this. I found out later she was an intuitive, an energy healer who had picked up on my empathic and intuitive nature. As she asked questions, I teared up very quickly and was unable to answer. I was blindsided. Since my mother had made her transition in 2012, I could not talk to her.

She said to me, so then, let's talk about her. Tell me something pleasant you recall. I cried and shared about the cookie giving five-foot Italian woman that flipped tables. This was a core memory where I was stuck. So, after this meeting, it dawned on me that it was time for me to heal the voice I had silenced for years.

We had a kid run house growing up in The Bronx, maybe it would serve me to do my inner work now and to talk, to use my voice. There are scenarios of my childhood that used to play over and over in my mind at the strangest times.

Somehow putting them on paper seems to equate to a release of some sort. If I just write about them, they will no longer visit me in my thoughts or my dreams, ever again.

UNTIL we know what's hidden, we cannot do our inner work to uncover and release it.

**Remember your superpowers:**
**IMAGINATION, INFLUENCE and INTUITION**.

# CHAPTER 12:
# THE MAGIC FORMULA / "I SEE YOU" poem

Now that I have the magic formula, what is it exactly? How do I use it? A few choices come to mind...you could choose to have faith over fear. You could choose to lose your attachment to the fear and find your bravery and you can trust your own voice.

I have a strong attraction to things unseen. This is why there are some things that I still, to this day, keep tucked away in my mind. The unseen, the intangible is where I create from. In essence, it's where I tap into my imagination, what influences me, and my intuition.

Remember, both fear and faith demand that belief in something we cannot see. I heard this recently for the first time, and it was as if the universe had answered my question. The one that I had not even asked before the chance meeting with the intuitive that I mentioned in the last chapter.

The magic formula isn't our pursuit of it, rather it's our experience of ourselves in energetic alignment with our calling.

Are these the moments in our human experience when our world stands still? When we trust and believe in ourselves, we need to do so despite our stories, and even more so, because of them.

Are these the moments when our faith is triumphant over our past and we get unshakable confidence?

No matter the argument or debate before you, I invite you to embrace your gifts. In these moments, being stuck is not possible, it cannot exist.

Life will push and pull you until you do your inner work and move through the invisibles. The ones that haunt you… the undone.

I have a truth bomb for you.

**THERE IS NO MAGIC FORMULA.**

Simply put, see the world through your own eyes and own it. It's like a force of nature. Your magic is like a force of nature. I compare it to rain that falls over the land whether we are ready for it or not, it does not need permission nor would it ever comply with us.

Forces of nature are like that. So then, why is it so hard for us humans to take on the same essence and be a force to be reckoned with while blazing our own unique and beautiful trail?

Maybe it isn't so hard, maybe it's simply a choice. It's the feeling that the magic is both near, yet distant. We are, in part content, yet restless.

We acknowledge there is still work to do and that the next step to take requires an open mind and heart.

Every human being wants to be seen, heard and loved...these are basic human needs for each one of us to thrive.

Take a moment and reflect on the gift of these simple, yet magical truths.

The following page is a poem written by my dear friend and colleague, Cassandra Lennox, author/writer/speaker, poet-extraordinaire:

## ***I SEE YOU***

I see you –
Beyond the external, behind the smile.

I see you –
Through adversity and every trial.

Far beyond, behind and below,
Your dreams and hopes, the depths of your soul.

I see the light that shines in the dark,
In the bleakest night, it ignites a spark.

I see the dreamer, the creator, the rhyme.
A legacy in the making to stand the test of time.

A story to be told, the pages await.
Why settle for good when you know you'll be great?

I see you –
Pure. Honest and true.
But what matters most…
Is that YOU see YOU.

## PART OF YOU SEEING YOU, IS GETTING TO KNOW YOURSELF!

## CHAPTER 13:
## PERSONAL POWER STATEMENT

This is an example of a "Personal Power Statement" that I wrote for myself long before **The Pathfinder Code®** ever evolved. This was the "writing on the wall" of the vision in my mind's eyes. I thought it appropriate to share here in this book and invite you to create your own! The creation of this statement has brought me to tears many times. When you create your own, I promise, that you too, will experience the emotions, as well as the release!

**YOU SEE, HOW YOU SPEAK TO YOURSELF, ABOUT YOURSELF, MATTERS.**

## HOW TO WRITE YOUR OWN:

Create your Personal Power Statement for your unique vision for your business! Just follow my lead and replace my words with your own! You can Google "power words" and start a list of your own. Take your time and do not hold back! Just keep writing!

## "PERSONAL POWER STATEMENT"

I am on a magical journey to impact thousands of lives.

I inspire others to awaken their mindset and heart space where all things are new.

My creative influence is my true calling.

Today I embrace my inner desires to be artistic, vivacious and notoriously brave.

I use my heart and hands to unleash the colors of the brighter world I yearn for every day.

I define who I am by my own intuitive terms, not by what is expected of me.

Today I surrender to my need to surround myself with beauty in every form.

I am that person that I did not have to support me; I am the healer of my being.

I refuse to spend my days doing anything not aligned with my purpose.

My passion for self-expression, creativity and empowering others is an unfolding of the perfect opportunities to bring myself and others, wealth, health and happiness.

Small victories are the path to my big dreams coming true.

## IT HAS ALL BEEN DONE BEFORE, BUT NOT BY ME

I am that woman who does not need validation by anyone.

I do things that make me smile.

My life's challenges are the catalyst for my success.

My happy place is where my passion resides and I choose to live there

My mindset is a vibrational match for what I want.

I ask for what I want and it shows up every day.

So it is, and so it will be.

## CHAPTER 14:
## VISUAL DISCOVERY TOOLS

What I would like to introduce you to in this chapter is the science behind The Pathfinder Code® Intuitive Art Reading, a visual discovery technique I created to help my clients release hidden emotional and energetic blocks. There is far more to the depth of what the reading uncovers, I will save that for my next book or your personal reading with me!

As a visual artist, I stumbled upon a secret language that was the catalyst for my own personal transformation. I discovered that I could "read" images and co-create through spoken words to help other people find their next right steps and path.

This is how The Pathfinder Code: Powered by Intuition and Creativity® evolved! I know it sounds crazy but it's true! I started to fuse the findings from intuitive art readings to map out a direction to help my coaching clients' clear emotional blocks and get

unstuck in their life, relationships, careers and business.
In the zone of your imagination, creativity and intuition, no thoughts exist, it's just the pathway between your heart and brain connection, where all that is unseen, can be seen, honored, addressed and released!

You too can develop a new modality or process to help your people, when you work with me to help you bring your ideas to life!

*Here is an excerpt from my website that describes this magical, block busting visual discovery technique:*

**What is an Intuitive Art reading?**

The "Intuitive Art Reading" is a transformative process and has helped my clients get unstuck and start the process of moving forward very quickly because of the deep connection created during our time together. The creation of art is intuitive, it is also an "energy signature" and "blueprint" of your awareness (who you are, how you feel, process emotions and situations) that can be interpreted through a "reading" to help you uncover and release hidden blocks that are physical, mental, emotional and spiritual.

**How will I benefit from an intuitive reading?**

Some people have greater difficulty getting unstuck, moving forward and releasing blocks. They have deep rooted hidden blocks that have held them captive for years. How could they move forward when they do not know what it is that's blocking them?

What they do know is that they feel "off" at times and unable to pinpoint the cause.

The Intuitive Art Reading is an "alternative personal growth process" that I share to help others break through stubborn blocks and forge a new "pathway". This pathway is unique and meant just for them, so they can then express and uncover what words cannot convey.

**What will it feel like after I have an intuitive reading?**

While this is unique to every person, you may find yourself feeling more focused, energetic, joyful and purposeful. Clients have shared with me that over time, the words, images, people and memories that had previously triggered them no longer had an emotional charge. The art you create is your "map" to your new path.

If you are wondering if you need to be "creative" in order to participate in or benefit from this type of intuitive reading, know that all you need is to be open and curious to get the most out of it!

**Are you going to show me how to do the "art" project during my reading?**

You will receive an instructional video, you will then do the exercise, on your own, then email me a picture of your art in advance of our session. I will then review your pictures on our call together and relay the message that came through to me for you, to give you the guidance you need based upon what I see in the picture.

**Why do I have to create art for this reading?**

The creation of art is an energetic blueprint and signature that can be interpreted through an intuitive reading.

**Will I have access to a recording of our session?**

Yes. When we start our reading, I will ask you for your permission to record it so I can send it to you.

**How often should I be getting intuitive readings like this?**

This is unique to your individual needs and the support system you have in place. My clients know I am available to assist them and can schedule a session anytime. After your first reading with me give yourself some time to process what we uncovered, and see, if over time, questions evolve.

**Why the readings provide lasting results:**

Your thoughts and words trigger emotions that reinforce your beliefs about yourself, whether they are positive or negative, past, present or pre-worry about the future.

The emotions run pathways that target your subconscious mind and specific places in our bodies. These are the places in your body where you hold and harness your personal power.

These are also the places that hold the limiting beliefs where you question your self-worth, confidence and value.

Because the subconscious mind (ego/intellect) shows these emotions the same way, every single time, this is where the notion of getting to know yourself intimately comes into play.

The intuitive art readings forge a new pathway and uncovers emotional blocks that have no symptoms, that lie hidden, yet those experiencing the reading do recall having received the signs to what is uncovered in the reading.

**How my clients use the findings in the readings:**

They reconnect with aspects of themselves that were hidden, including childhood memories and at times, ancestry and hidden emotional blocks that help them identify exactly where they are stuck.

They learn the lesson of identifying the cause of negative self-talk and better understand the signs that show up to alert them of a disconnect in their heart and brain connection.

The reading uncovers where they are energetically when they created the art.

Using the example of the reading, it's one method of forging a new pathway through energy work. The goal is to become more self-aware by honoring where you are, what you need to address (the blocks) and the type of help you need to achieve your goals.

Sometimes people are not ready to look at the signs that show up. If only they knew that the clues were there solely to get them to pause, quiet themselves and pay attention.

If you don't take time to pause, you bypass the opportunity to understand the signs. The nudges or gut instincts can come and go very quickly. It could be months or even years before you sense their presence. It's unique as each individual. The soul consequences are not fully understanding yourself by not addressing why you feel "off". It's very easy and common to become desensitized to your own mind chatter (negative self-talk).

In order to change something, you must first become aware of it. This is the beginning.

## ART AND SCIENCE

In "How Colors Affect You: What Science Reveals", taught by design expert and professor William Lidwell of the University of Houston, he found:

"That the power of color to create environments and achieve a range of visual goals were central to this course is the expanse of information about how colors work on our brains to steer our thoughts and actions. You'll go behind the scenes and examine the fascinating experiments and case studies that scientists have used to uncover what they know about color. And you'll finally understand the (often hidden) significance behind the colors of your everyday life. Lidwell, goes on to say, "A must-have course for corporate leaders, design professionals, marketers, and anyone else who communicates visually, *How Colors Affect You* tells you everything you need to know about the science of color and its impact on all aspects of human experience. These lectures will give you a beautiful new perspective on color - one rooted in credible scientific knowledge and not popular myth."

Another study, Art Therapy, Journal of the American Art Therapy Association, titled "Reduction of Cortisol Levels and Participants Responses Following Art making" by Girjia Kaimal, Kendra Ray and Juan Munoz, found that 45 minutes of creative activity significantly lessens stress in the body, regardless of artistic experience or talent.

This study supports this notion of how creating art reduces stress and allows individuals to "release" hidden emotional blocks.

One of the visual discovery techniques in The Pathfinder Code® Intuitive Art Reading give participants an opportunity to de-stress and release emotions; once the art is created through my instructional training and breathwork, clients produce what I have coined as an "energy signature blueprint" through the process of what is released onto the art paper!

This process has birthed amazing breakthroughs and clarity!

# CHAPTER 15:
# YOUR NEW NOW

I see you, in your "new now" with eyes wide open. Do you?

Remember those lists you made in the earlier chapters?

You were invited to create your vision statement, mission statement, your core values, core super colors and a "Power Statement". You may have an idea of the ideal client that you'd like to serve. You may have an idea of the products and services in your business. That is, if you did the exercises and took the action steps I suggested in the earlier chapters; you might even have that social proof that you need!

As you work with people and deliver on the promises you're making, and the promise you're keeping, you must remain energetically aligned with your calling. When everything comes together, the way I know it will for you, if you followed all my steps, (and I mean every single one!) You've got to decide, commit, and take action. And then you've got to lather, rinse, repeat. Why? Because never being talked out of your magic, ever again, means you must "own" your power and your magic and have a crystal-clear intention! That is, if you truly desire answers to your burning questions and yearning to unleash your magic!

Believe in yourself because faith and your natural knowing live in this space.

I'll repeat it again so it nudges you to work through the emotions you may not want to face:

Remember to deal with those invisibles or they will haunt you.

Creating the business, you really want is not as hard as you think it is. You start out with the idea, you have challenges, you meet people along the way that are going to help you get to the place you need and want to be.

Then, at some point you cross the threshold where you start acquiring knowledge you didn't have before. Then you start having trials and at times feel somewhat defeated. This is because you're acquiring new skills. After that, you get to that middle ground. This is where I would call on the "create and destroy" process that artists utilize to master their craft. It's in this part of the journey that you will experience a rebirth of your self-image and perspective.

Next comes the revelation of "Hey, maybe I'm kind of good at this"!

Somewhere between there and here, you will experience the process of change I mentioned earlier in the book. Why? Because you've started to implement the things that you've been learning. This is the point of acceptance where you begin to acquire the energetic boost you need to push your own boundaries. Picture yourself in the situations that you want to be in. Picture yourself turned on and lit up. Picture yourself living in an enchanted world, one where you're living in your new now with your eyes wide open. You have created the business you really want and your life and happiness factor are like Christmas in July.

There is an art to everything. However, there's one thing I know for sure...you are reading this book because you are being called to take giant leaps in order to really see into yourself.

**See yourself = Set Yourself Free**

You've got to be a warrior, you've got to be on fire, you've got to imagine the utopia within and that your new now is waiting for you.

Now you're at a point on this journey where you've returned to your authentic self, you know what feels like "home", reinvented yourself and so much more. You have played hard and you have rocked it. You're the happiest ever, you're a wild agent of change... your passport has been stamped and off you go!

The key to an extraordinary life is quite literally, creating the life you desire, and riding uncertainty like a wave.

# CHAPTER 16:
# YOUR NEXT RIGHT STEPS

When it comes to unleashing your magic in the world, it's always a good idea to have a support system! Although I find myself most weeks being a ***one- woman social media team,*** I know when to reach out for help!

Make technology your friend, as a Pathfinder, you seek out and explore new ways of being and accomplishing your goals. This means embracing your creativity and organizational skills!

Here is a quick overview of what you need to do to get set up online! It is very empowering to learn how to run the technology for your business. Down the road, you can get help as your scale your business.

## WEBSITE AND RELATED TECHNOLOGY – YOU NEED TO KNOW

This is where the public gets to meet you, read about your background, your services, the praise and reviews others have given you, and where they register to work with you.

While you are human and need your beauty rest, your website is 24/7 billboard for your online one stop shop!

~**Selecting your url**: Once you have all of the work done laid out this book and know the name for your business, you can visit www.GoDaddy.com or if you plan to self-mange your website, an easy platform to use is www.Wix.com.

~**Business email:** create a professional email (yourname@____.com)

On your site, I suggest you set up the following pages:

~ **Meet** (your name) this is the same as an "**About**" page. I would recommend creating a story video that is under two minutes that introduces who you are and why you do what you do. Invite others into your world. Share briefly a few lines about what you do, however, the page should be clear on what the benefits are for someone choosing to work with you.

~ **Services** (while registration is on your Work with Me Page, it's a good idea to give details so your next rock star client knows what to expect, you can tell the story here).

~ **Work with Me** (I would use this page and integrate a platform like www.Calendly.com

this is a one stop for potential clients to fill out an intake form, book an appointment and pay for your services. This service includes an auto-responder that confirms and sends follow up emails.

~ **Reviews/Testimonials**– this page is for all of the social proof you have or will collect. I take screenshots with my phone and upload them to my website.

~ **Contact**-this page should include a form for visitors to share their name, phone, email and a question stating: "How can I help you?" with several lines for them to type onto. It can also include a FREE Gift and an invite to join your email list.

~**Social Media buttons**-here are the ones that rule, You Tube, Facebook, Linkedin, Instagram, Twitter and Pinterest.

~**Automating your Emails**: this is used for lead magnets like free gifts, PDFs. Mp3's, etc., while there are many to choose from I use www.Mailchimp.com

~**Zoom videoconference**- like most entrepreneurs, you are conducting sessions, trainings, webinars, workshops and more virtually. Zoom is an excellent source for this service.

~**Canva** has been a reliable and easy to learn resource for creating graphics for posts and more. www.canva.com

~**Content/Copywriting** is the creation of content that you use in your social media and share publicly. Copywriting speaks to the tonality or persuasive aspects of how it pertains to and attracts your ICA to seeing you as the solution to their problems. The tone of your content should be phrased so it is aligned with your core values and consistent with your brand, across platforms. When posting quotes or content from other sources, always give credit. ~**Distribution, publishing and marketing your content**. I would suggest you start with one social media platform, one ideal client profile, one method of converting clients (a discovery call) or consult, depending on your line of work. This is so you can test the waters to see what works.

## SOCIAL MEDIA PRESENCE

No matter which platform is your primary, and you should have one, this is where most of your ideal clients hang out. For instance, let's take **Facebook**, which happens to be my expertise.

There is your **personal timeline**, this is what I call the *organic funnel* for your business and should be set up properly. Your **bio** should indicate who you are, what you do and the results you get for your clients.

Your Facebook **banner** on all of your pages, both personal and business is free advertising for your **Facebook Group**!

Your **Facebook Group** is where you invite your ideal clients and like-minded folks to create a warm audience.

Your **Facebook Business Page** is where you run ads, it also verifies your identity and your business. Visitors can also leave your business and you a personal "**recommendation**".

These recommendations are social proof you will need to continue to acquire as you build your business.

Credibility, integrity and transparency are everything.

## SALES AND MARKETING

~**Organic Leads and Sales**: It's a good idea to study and learn how to create your own copy. I promise it will serve you. Then as you grow your business you can get help. There are methods to getting organic leads without an expensive funnel. This is something I personally use and teach my clients.

## THE KEY TO SALES

Building rapport and relationships are the number one goal.

Getting in front of your ideal client and getting to know them and care about what they want and need is crucial to your success.

You may have heard that people do business with those they know, like and trust.

I am personally very generous with my clients. It is my job to see into them, those things they do not observe about themselves that are the key to their breakthroughs.

If you are not all in, your clients will know it and will not stick around.

Back in Chapter 5, I provided you with a sample of a Marketing Research post that you could make

your own and use to attract those people that you believe are your ideal clients, ask to interview them in exchange for a 30 minute chat with you where you guide them in some area of their life or business.
This costs you nothing but your time and research.

If you are uncomfortable with "selling" it's something, know that for most people this is a limiting belief and fear sourced by your conscious mind (ego/intellect). If you take my advice about building rapport and relationships, your services will sell themselves. I am not taking light that there is always some persuasion that will need to take place, however, if you believe in your ability to help another human, and it's a good fit, that will be conveyed and felt during your conversation.

If it's not a good fit you will be very aware of that too!

Just start, stop dwelling in what you have cooked up in your mind. There are lots of stories in your head, some of them aren't even yours! Imagine that, letting something someone else said or imprinted on you at some point in your life, influence your confidence and cause you to doubt your ability to deliver the magic that person that has been waiting for you to show up so they could get the help they need.

You see, many people have a way of developing a kindred connection in a very short period of time.

What I mean by this, is that, you can have five people deliver the same message on a product or service and you only resonate with one of the sales reps. This is what I am referring to when I say, there is only one you, and you are the only one that can deliver what you do to help that other human waiting....for whatever it is to be conveyed, so they can make the purchase they need to enhance their life and grow.

Imagine, you gave up and didn't take the time to rediscover your magic, didn't align your path and calling, and didn't bring your ideas to life. That's right, that person would not be getting the benefit of your gifts that they need to feel whole.

**REMEMBER YOUR POWER, THIS IS YOUR MAGIC.**

# CHAPTER 17:
# MINDSET MAGIC – THE HACKS

It's time to **grab that pen and paper**. This time, it's to write an affirmation or mantra that you will look at every day that you're in business. <u>This is a necessary mindset hack</u>. Use a post-it, a white board, or whatever works for you personally.

Here is one that might help you with *money blocks*, asking for and being paid what you are worth:

**"I attract new clients that have money to pay me what I am worth because what I teach is going to change their life."**

Here is another example of using the notion of "**Trusting the Process**" and how it can help you work through self-doubt that might creep in long after you have rediscovered your magic.

**MINDSET HACK EXAMPLE:**

Write clear affirmations that are useful in implementing what you need to convey in order to believe in yourself.

**CONS EXAMPLE:**

I need to get more confident and committed.

I need to stop procrastinating.

I need to stop comparing myself to others.

**AFFIRMATIONS:**

In order to speed up the process, I relax.

I am content with where I am and do not need to see the mountain top along the journey there.

I am open to relaxing in this process and I do not need to over-analyze everything.

I do not need to see the whole picture and I trust the process that the next and perfect steps are being revealed to me in the right timing, as is the right services for me to offer.

A different business requires a different mindset

Things that I am to offer as a service are unfolding in the right way, at the right time, and are revealed to me to unveil my right journey.

Its ok that I do not have all the answers.

I am content with where I am and the process of revealing.

The right forks in the road will be revealed to me at the right and perfect time.

This isn't rocket science, I am relaxed and not analytical.

I can do this easily.

The universe is revealing signs that I need to get the right combination of businesses up and running and the next steps are being revealed to me in divine timing.

Trust the process.

The world is letting me know my services are seen and very much needed for healing the planet and its people.

I am confident that the right business model is being revealed to me.

I am capable and confident and able to turn my skills into useful and applicable implementation tools.

**The question asked:**

How do I tap into "restarting" on my business when I've been away from it for a few days or week because I work full time? Sometimes I feel like it takes me a long time.

**Answer:** My 60-70% is thorough enough-no analyzing needed. Trust the Process.

So, as you can see given the examples here, mindset hacks can be great tools!

**To have the success and freedom that entrepreneurship brings once you have built your empire, you simply must commit to be your own best friend and cheerleader.**

These mindset hacks and those you will create are daily reminders that you shall read every day, so you remember exactly what your magic is and why you do, what you do,

Yes, what you do, may have been done before, but not by YOU! There is only one YOU.

# CHAPTER 18: SUSTAINABLE MAGIC

You made it! Throughout this book, I have given you the intuitive nudges that came to me, and the creative framework to energetically align your path and calling! Now, I know you have some questions and some ideas that have been dancing around in your head that you want to bring to life!

That is what this last chapter "Sustainable Magic" is all about! The word *Sustainable* is defined as "the ability to be maintained at a certain rate or level." Now while this book provides you with the tools and strategies to get started in your entrepreneurial and personal growth journey, I want you to know that my help doesn't end here!

I would encourage you to join the conversation in ***The Pathfinder Code® for Heart Centered Entrepreneurs, Creatives and Coaches.***

The reason for this is that we have tremendous amounts more work to do!

This strategies in this book work no matter where you are, especially if you are just getting started. In my group, I cover more in-depth topics and trainings.

I do this to ensure you are supported!

I believe that if I give away as much value as possible, the ideal heart-centered aspiring entrepreneurs will reach out and be excited to work with me to co-create their next right steps.

At this moment, I am getting an intuitive nudge and feel as though you are one of those heart-centered individuals.

To make this easy for you, here is the link to spend more one-on-one time with me.

https://calendly.com/coachlilynava/rediscoveryourmagic

Yes, knowing that you came to me from the link in this book will make a big difference because you will have gained the value of the experience, tools and strategies you learned!

**ALL YOU NEED TO DO NOW IS TO CONTINUE DOING YOUR INNER WORK ...**

**AND YOU WILL START SEEING THE RESULTS!**

# CONCLUSION:

***The ones who are crazy enough to think they can change the world are the ones that do. ~ Steve Jobs***

When I finally sat down to write this book, it was prompted by several things. First, I had always wanted to write a book and started on two of them about a year or so ago. Second, an amazing coach showed up in my world who took myself and a tribe of other entrepreneurs on a "30 days to Print" Training. I knew I always had a book in me. But, 30 days?

The only thing I knew for sure was that a portal had opened, a guide appeared who challenged all of us to see beyond any limiting beliefs of writing and publishing a book. So yes, this book was written in 30 days. It did take a bit longer to edit and publish. However, this is a prime example of how much one can get done with a clear intention and a laser focus.

While I had guidelines on how to write a book, I just started talking on paper and never stopped, until over 24,000 words later.

For years, I have talked about how creating art is a magical and healing experience.

I have also talked about how so many people have been talked out of their magic, meaning doing the thing that lights them up, from the inside out.

The true meaning behind this book and the notion to REDISCOVER YOUR MAGIC is to teach you to advocate for yourself, with yourself, first. This is not a typo.

You see, my theory in The Pathfinder Code® is that once you uncover hidden emotional blocks, shine a light on them, bid them farewell, find your voice and harness the power unleashed in your life and business, you can handle any challenge that comes your way.

If there is one thing, I hope you take away from this book, in addition to knowing that you have been nudged to embrace your "Pathfinder" instincts, it's this:

**IT'S YOUR TIME AND IT'S YOUR TURN TO REDISCOVER YOUR MAGIC AND UNLEASH THE GIFTS THAT WERE GIFTED TO YOU AT BIRTH.**

It's also to remind you to have faith in a universe and source that has your ultimate best interest in mind. Whatever this looks like for you, use that faith and apply it to everything in your life, with all your heart and soul. Ask for the help you need, every day. Trust that what you need will always show up at the perfect and divine timing.

Know that your magic is sustainable! I hope I will have the opportunity to meet you in person one day. I cannot wait to hear how you energetically aligned your path and calling and how you rediscovered your magic!

Remember, there were gifts bestowed upon you before you took your very first breath.

You are not alone in this journey and have the benefit of this newfound knowledge and **The Pathfinder Code®** tribe to support you!

I am so glad you made it here to the end of this book, I want to celebrate this milestone with you. I say this, as I read somewhere that most people only read the first 17 pages of a book!

How could this be true? I am ecstatic that this isn't true for you! How could it be?

You are someone that has embraced, rediscovered and unleashed the magic that lives in your heart space!

You are someone very special.

You know there is more out there for you.

You know that your calling was divinely assigned and that you were predestined for greatness!

This is your beautiful soul journey and it's just beginning.

**THE END**

Yes of course, while all books must end, rediscovering your magic does not end!

As an intuitive, I am getting a nudge that you are wanting to know more. See my invitation to YOU on the next page!

## YOU ARE INVITED!

Hello Beautiful Soul!

It's your turn, it's your time. Did you know...that heart-centered people from all walks of life, just like you, are longing to energetically align their path with their calling and bring their ideas to life?

The Pathfinder Code® it is a soulful empowerment and alternative coaching program that has helped extraordinary folks, ready to bust through the invisible barriers to decode their blocks, get unstuck and harness their power to influence and change lives, starting with their own!

I see you, and I want to help you find your next right path, the one "meant just for you" so your intuition, self-awareness and confidence are bigger than your fears- so you can lead in your life, relationships and your career.

So, get in here and join The Pathfinder Code® Community:

**The Pathfinder Code for Heart-Centered Entrepreneurs, Creatives and Coaches**

https://www.facebook.com/groups/thepathfindercode/

I would be honored to help you! In case you missed the link to spend more time with me one-on-one, here it is https://calendly.com/coachlilynava/rediscoveryourmagic

To learn more about the programs I am currently offering: **www.thepathfindercode.com**

I look forward to the opportunity to connect with you and see how you are doing with rediscovering your magic and aligning your path and your calling!

Email me at **lily@thepathfindercode.com** and tell me how you are using this book to make a difference in your life and the world! My Heart to Yours,

Lily Nicholson

## ABOUT THE AUTHOR

Lily Nicholson is best known is for her intuitive insight, creativity and magnetic energy. She is the creator and founder of The Pathfinder Code: Powered by Intuition and Creativity®, a soulful empowerment and alternative personal growth coaching program.

Lily is known as an Intuitive Life Coach who empowers aspiring entrepreneurs to "own" their voice, personal power, advocate for themselves, to bridge the gap to their desired destination and cocreate bringing their ideas to life.

Lily is also an advocate and coach for women seeking to find their life path, no matter where they are in their journey.

Lily's organic practices have evolved over the past few years and are now the substance of her signature coaching program.

This program provides the opportunity for her clients to have the experience of getting to know themselves intimately, owning their voice and becoming self-aware.

Once this initial inner work has taken place, they experience a deep dive to mesh their gift, talents and bring their ideas to life. This includes branding, identifying ideal clients and social media presence.

The end result is they are aligned with who they are authentically and energetically resulting in more personal freedom to just be themselves and navigate their life and careers on their own terms.

Lily has been a professional Visual Artist since 2005 and has owned and operated her creative business, as well as coached artists on the "Business of Art" helping them to step into their own creative visions for their art careers.

Her background in law has been a valuable resource in business ventures. Lily believes that every experience contributes to overall happiness and success in life.

**YOU CAN LEARN MORE ABOUT LILY AT**

www.thepathfindercode.com

www.lilynavagallery.com

**CONNECT WITH HER ON SOCIAL MEDIA AT:**

Facebook:

https://www.facebook.com/ThePathfinderCode/

Instagram:

https://www.instagram.com/thepathfindercode/

Linkedin:

https://www.linkedin.com/in/lilynavanicholson/

You Tube: Find me @Lily Nava-Nicholson.

## SOURCES


1. Zukav, Gary, "Soul Stories, https://www.amazon.com/SoulStories-Gary-Zukav/dp/0743206371
2. Peloso, Paul, Certified NLP Practitioner and Hypnotherapist, "The Process of Change", Founder of The Hypnotic Solution. https://www.thehypnoticsolution.com
3. Lidwell, William, University of Houston, "How Colors Affect You: What Science Reveals"  taught by design expert and professor https://www.parkablogs.com/content/review-howcolor-affects-you-what-science-reveals-craftsy
4. Leonard, Janick, "What is Heart Coherence and Why is it so Powerful?" https://wanderlust.com/journal/what-is-heartcoherence/
5. Cherry, Kenda, Gans, Steven, M.D., Color Psychology: Does it Affect How You Feel? https://www.verywellmind.com/colorpsychology-2795824

6. Girjia Kaimal, Kendra Ray and Juan Munoz, Art Therapy, Journal of the American Art Therapy Association, titled "Reduction of Cortisol Levels and Participants Responses Following Art Making" https://www.tandfonline.com/doi/full/10.1080/07421656.2016.1166832

7. Lennox, Cassandra. "I See You." The Inspiration Chain. May 1, 2019. https://cassandralennox.com

Made in the USA
Las Vegas, NV
15 November 2020

10939993R00098